Everything
BUG

What Kids Really Want to Know About Insects and Spiders

by
Cherie Winner

NORTHWORD PRESS
Chanhassen, Minnesota

Edited by Kristen McCurry
Designed by Brad Springer

Text © 2004 by Cherie Winner

Books for Young Readers
NorthWord Press
18705 Lake Drive East
Chanhassen, MN 55317
www.northwordpress.com

Photographs © 2004 provided by:
Brand X Pictures: cover, backcover (bee), pp. 1 (caterpillar, butterfly, ants), 4, 5,
6 (weevil), 7, 11, 14 (bee, crane fly, butterfly), 15 (beetle, ants, praying mantis,
butterfly), 24 (praying mantis), 26 (ants), 29 (flyswatter), 36 (spider), 37, 40, 60
(earwig); Fotosearch.com/Corbis: p. 46 (praying mantis); Fotosearch.com/Corel:
pp. 1 (bees), 3, 9 (bee, ladybugs), 12 (midges), 13, 20, 27, 28, 29 (fly close-up),
39, 42, 46 (caterpillar), 48, 59 (spider); Fotosearch.com/John Foxx: p. 29 (fly full
body); James E. Gerholdt/www.remarkablereptiles.com: p. 35 (black widow);
Getty Images: backcover (ladybug, spider, shield bug), pp. 6 (butterfly, children),
9 (hover fly), 10, 12 (hornets), 14 (spider, stinkbug), 15 (spider), 16, 17, 18, 19,
21, 22, 23, 24 (boy), 25, 26 (ant sandwich), 36 (boy), 38, 41, 44 (butterfly), 45
(moth), 53, 55, 56, 57, 58, 60 (dragonfly), 61, 62; Index Stock Imagery/
Elizabeth A. DeLaney: p. 54; Robert & Linda Mitchell: pp. 30, 33, 35 (brown
recluse), 44 (chrysalis), 45 (cocoon), 49, 51, 59 (cricket).

Library of Congress Cataloging-in-Publication Data
Winner, Cherie.
    Everything bug : what kids really want to know about insects and spiders /
by Cherie Winner.
        p. cm. — (Kids' FAQs)
    Summary: Presents twenty-five questions and answers about insects and
spiders, including why bugs are important, how long they've existed, and why
crickets make noise.
Includes biographical references (p. 62).
        ISBN 1-55971-890-9 (hardcover) — ISBN 1-55971-891-9 (softcover)
    1. Insects—Miscellanea—Juvenile literature. 2. Spiders—Miscellanea—
Juvenile literature.
    [1. Insects—Miscellanea. 2. Spiders—Miscellanea. 3. Questions and
answers.] I. Title.

QL467.2.W59 2004
595.7—dc21

                                                                    2003048761

Printed in Singapore
10 9 8 7 6 5 4 3 2 1

Acknowledgments

THE AUTHOR THANKS THE 4TH GRADERS AT SHELLEDY Elementary School in Fruita, Colorado, for their warm welcome and great questions; and Thomas R. Walla, Ph.D., Assistant Professor of Biology at Mesa State College in Grand Junction, Colorado, for his enthusiastic help in looking for answers.

Dedication

TO SHEBA, WHO HAS NEVER READ A BOOK, BUT WHO CAN read a trail and my moods better than anyone else I know.

—C. W.

contents

Beetles and butterflies are easy to tell apart, but with some bugs you need to take a closer look.

introduction

BUGS DO AMAZING THINGS. They walk on ceilings, build intricate webs, and always seem to know when you're having a picnic. You may think they're cool. You may think they're icky. Or maybe you think they're a little bit of both. Maybe you love butterflies, but hate mosquitoes. Maybe you marvel at dragonflies, but get the willies if you see a spider in your bathtub. I'm that way. I love animals, even creepy-crawly ones, but when ants run up my legs or caterpillars devour my tomato plants, I almost wish the bugs would all go away.

What if they did? Without insects and spiders, we'd have no bug bites or cobwebs, no malaria, and no crops ruined by locusts. But wait. Spiders and insects do a lot of good things, too. If they disappeared, many fish, frogs, and birds would starve. Old poop and dead animals would pile up around us. We'd have no apples, cotton, or pumpkins. Worst of all, we'd have no chocolate!

That settles it for me. For the sake of chocolate conservation, some young friends and I set off on a quest to learn more about bugs. Here are some of the questions we asked, starting with the most important.

Why wouldn't we have chocolate if bugs disappeared?

Chocolate comes from seeds of the cacao plant, and in order to make seeds, cacao flowers must be pollinated by insects. The same goes for most other plants. Name your favorite fruit—or vegetable, if you have a favorite vegetable—and it's likely that bugs have something to do with pollinating it. Without insects to carry their pollen from one plant to another, these plants couldn't make fruit, seeds, or baby plants. Of course, the insects don't know they're pollinating. They just visit the plants looking for food, and pollen happens to stick to them as they travel from flower to flower.

Bees are the most famous pollinators, but other kinds of insects do the job, too. Sometimes many insects visit a flower and it's hard to figure out which ones carry pollen. With cacao, tiny flies called midges probably pollinate the flowers. Ants, wild bees, and tiny oval insects called aphids might also help.

Bumblebees, beetles, and flies are just a few of the insects that pollinate flowers.

Were insects and spiders here in the time of dinosaurs?

By the time dinosaurs showed up about 200 million years ago, insects and spiders had already been here for ages. The oldest fossils of insects and spiders are about 400 million years old. These prehistoric bugs looked a lot like modern insects and spiders, with a few differences. For one thing, many bugs were much bigger then. A fossil from 370 million years ago shows a dragonfly with

wings that spread more than 2 feet (61 cm) wide.

Another difference is that the first insects didn't have wings. And since the insects couldn't fly, the spiders didn't make big, prey-catching webs to snag them like the ones we see today. Instead, ancient spiders caught insects by stalking or ambushing them.

Around 315 million years ago, some kinds of insects evolved wings. When dinosaurs finally appeared, millions of insects and spiders prowled the lush forests. Cockroaches scuttled along the ground, giant dragonflies droned through the air, and intricate spiderwebs hung from towering ferns.

When dinosaurs became extinct about 65 million years ago, many other animals and plants disappeared, too. Dinosaurs never made a comeback, but spiders and insects were able to recover. Today they thrive in almost every habitat on Earth.

Hornets guard their mud nest, midges swarm above a bush, and a diving beetle seeks prey underwater.

Is there any place on Earth where bugs don't live?

Insects and spiders live in just about every habitat you can imagine—in lakes and streams, at the tops of trees, on high mountains, deep underground, in the hottest deserts, and even in parts of the Arctic. Only a few bugs live on the oceans. And, if you really want to live "bug free," consider moving to the North or South Pole, where there are no bugs at all.

How many kinds of insects and spiders are there?

We live in a "golden age" of insects. About 75 percent of all the species of animals on Earth are insects—almost a million species! We also enjoy the company of at least 37,000 kinds of spiders. By contrast, there are only about 10,000 species of birds.

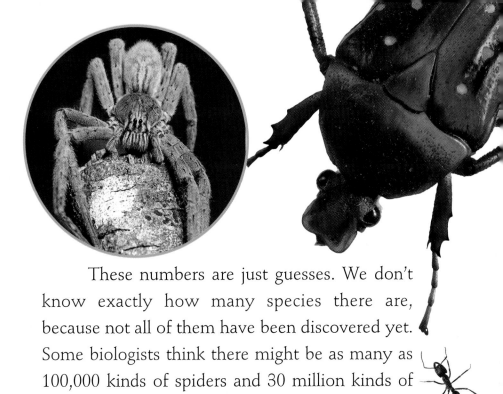

These numbers are just guesses. We don't know exactly how many species there are, because not all of them have been discovered yet. Some biologists think there might be as many as 100,000 kinds of spiders and 30 million kinds of insects on Earth. Most of the unknown species live in tropical rain forests in Central America, South America, and Africa. These forests are home to so many different kinds of animals that new species are found every week. Unfortunately, many species have already become extinct, as the rain forests have been cut down to make room for farms, houses, and roads.

Insects: six legs, two antennae, no pedipalps

What's the difference between insects and spiders?

The differences that are easiest to see are that insects have six legs and two antennae, while spiders have eight legs and no antennae. Every

Spiders: eight legs, no antennae, two pedipalps (shown in the middle in this head-on view)

spider also has two leg-like parts called pedipalps that it uses for handling food and for mating.

Both insects and spiders belong to a group of animals called arthropods. This huge group also includes millipedes, centipedes, ticks, scorpions, daddy longlegs, and crustaceans (such as crabs and crayfish). They all carry their skeleton on the outside of their body, like a thin shell, and their bodies and legs are divided up into segments.

A spiderweb sparkles with dewdrops in the early morning light.

Aren't spiders also different because they make webs?

Not quite. Spiders are famous for their silken webs, but some insects also make silk, which they use for many purposes. For example, moth caterpillars make their cocoons out of silk. The silkworm moth makes a special kind of silk. Long ago, people in China discovered that by boiling silkworm cocoons, they could unwind the silk threads to weave into cloth. Unfortunately, no one has found a way to remove the silk threads without killing the silkworm inside.

Once it reaches adulthood, a silkworm moth no longer makes silk.

Young caddisflies do more than make silk. They actually spin webs. They live in streams where they hang nets of silk between pebbles. Their nets snag plankton and other tiny foods that drift by.

An argiope spider wraps a butterfly in silk.

Another reason the answer to this question is "not quite" is that while all spiders make silk, not all of them make webs. Spiders use silk for many jobs. They wrap their prey in it to keep it fresh, like nature's sandwich baggie. They also weave snug pouches around their eggs to keep them moist and safe from predators.

Some spiders do very unusual—and pretty amazing—things with their silk. The diving water spider makes a miniature "diving bell," a chamber filled with air that allows the spider to live underwater. The spider only leaves its diving-bell home to capture tiny fish or tadpoles. On land, trapdoor spiders dig a burrow in the ground, line it with silk, and make a silken "trapdoor" cover for it. When a prey insect walks by, the spider rushes out, grabs the insect, and drags it back into the burrow.

The bolas spider has an even niftier trick. It pulls out a silk thread a few inches long and puts a drop of gooey fluid on the end. Then the spider waits, holding its thread in one foreleg. When a moth flies close enough, the spider throws its thread at the moth, like a cowboy trying to lasso a cow. If the drop of glue hits the moth, it sticks, and the spider hauls in its dinner.

Why don't spiders stick to their own webs?

They walk on tiptoe. Really! Insects get stuck because they walk on the web flat-footed. That gives the web more surface to stick to.

Spiders have another secret for not getting stuck. They make different kinds of silk. Some strands are very sticky, and others aren't sticky at all. The spiders know which threads are easiest to walk on. Their prey don't.

What are the biggest insects and spiders?

● ● ● ● ● ● ● ● ● ● ● ● ●

What are the smallest?

Some stick insects reach almost 15 inches (38.1 cm) long but are very skinny. The luna moth, cecropia moth, and regal moth have bodies only 2 to 3 inches (5.1 to 7.6 cm) long but with wingspans of up to 6 inches (15.2 cm). Among spiders, tarantulas hold the size record. The body of the goliath tarantula of South America is about 4 inches (10.2 cm) long, and its legs spread 10 inches (25.4 cm) wide. That's far enough to wrap halfway around your head!

Big bugs really get our attention, but most insects and spiders are less than a quarter of an inch (6 mm) long. Some wasps are only about one one-hundredth of an inch (0.25 mm) long.

This picture of a tarantula is ALMOST as big as the real thing.

Why doesn't a bug grow to be as big as a dog?

Despite what we see in horror movies, no insect or spider could ever grow big enough to devour a whole city. It's simply impossible. That's because their skeleton is on the outside of their body. This "exoskeleton" works well for small creatures. However, if a bug grew to be as large as a St. Bernard (or even a cocker spaniel) its exoskeleton would tear open like an overloaded grocery sack. Even if the exoskeleton could grow thick and strong enough to support a humongous bug, it would be so heavy the bug probably wouldn't be able to move.

What do spiders and insects eat?

All spiders are predators, which means they catch and eat other animals, mostly insects. A few species are big enough to catch lizards, birds, tadpoles, or fish.

Insects eat all kinds of things. Some insects are predators, like the praying mantis that nabs other insects with its long, spiny forelegs. Some are plant-eaters, like the boll weevils that ruin cotton crops; or parasites, like fleas and lice, which feed off other animals but usually don't kill them. Some insects are scavengers that eat dead things, like fruit flies that swarm over rotting fruit, and carrion beetles that munch on the carcasses of deer and other animals. And some insects, like the cockroaches that live in kitchen cupboards, will eat just about anything.

There's no escape for an insect caught by a hungry praying mantis.

These ants aren't real, but real ones will find your sandwich if you leave it outside.

Why are ants so good at finding food?

The places people pick for picnics are usually close to where ants live, and if you put food anywhere in their neighborhood, they will find it. Ants are always on the lookout for new sources of food. They are also great teamworkers. If one ant stumbles across a plate of fried chicken, he scurries home and tells the whole ant colony about it. He leaves a scent trail the other ants can follow to reach the fried chicken. And once they find that, they are sure to find the potato salad, the baked beans, and the soda pop, too.

Why do people put ladybugs in their gardens?

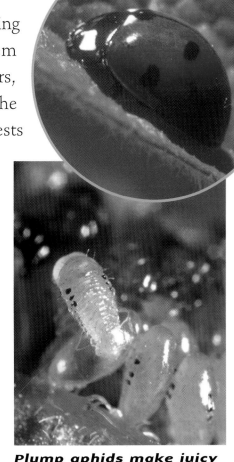

Ladybugs just love eating aphids. That makes them very popular with gardeners, because aphids are one of the most destructive garden pests around. They poke their sharp snouts into a leaf or stem and suck the plant's sap. This makes the plant sick and sometimes even kills it. Setting ladybugs loose in your yard is a good way to battle the aphids without using insecticides. To a ladybug, a rosebush crowded with aphids looks like an all-you-can-eat buffet.

Plump aphids make juicy treats for ladybugs.

Why are grasshoppers such good jumpers?

A grasshopper can jump 50 times its own length. That's like you leaping to the top of the Statue of Liberty!

Grasshoppers jump better than most other insects because their hind legs are longer and have thick, powerful muscles. (Most insects have scrawny legs.) But the real secret to being such a great jumper isn't in their legs. Grasshoppers jump so much better than we do because they are so much smaller than we are. Smaller animals can just jump higher and farther than larger animals.

Watch two dogs jump up into the air. A little one like a Chihuahua can jump several times its own height, but a big one like a Great Dane can barely jump as high as it is tall. The Chihuahua has smaller muscles, but he also has a lot less weight to lift—so his muscles can launch him higher.

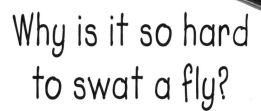

Why is it so hard to swat a fly?

Flies can feel the breeze from a flyswatter or rolled-up magazine zooming toward them. They also have huge eyes that give them a wraparound view of the world. They can see your flyswatter coming from just about any direction. Then, they have rapid-fire reflexes and springy legs that let them dart away before you even know they're gone.

A close-up of a fly's large eyes shows the wrap-around effect.

Only male crickets chirp. That's how they claim territory and find a mate.

Chirp

Chirp

Chirp *Chirp* *Chirp* *Chirp*

How do crickets make that chirping sound?

When a male cricket rubs his front wings together, a hard strip on each wing scrapes across ridges on the other wing. It's a lot like the sound you make when you drag your fingernail along the teeth of a comb, only much faster. Female crickets don't chirp. They don't have the ridges on their front wings that males have.

Male crickets chirp to proclaim their territory and attract a mate. One kind of loud chirp tells other male crickets, "This is my place. Stay away!" A different loud chirp tells female crickets, "Here I am, ready to mate!" When a female comes close, the male cricket chirps more softly. He wants to coax her in without letting other males know she is there. It's like whispering, "Pssst! Over here!"

What makes lightning bugs light up?

Lightning bugs, or fireflies, have a "light organ" in their abdomen that contains special chemicals that mix together to produce light. The skin over that part of the abdomen is transparent, so it makes a sort of window that lets the light shine through. Most firefly lights are yellow, but they can also be green, blue, or orange, depending on the species.

Lightning bugs light up to attract a mate. The female stays on the ground while the male cruises along, flashing in a way that advertises what species he belongs to. He flashes at a certain height above the ground, and in a specific pattern. For example, one kind of firefly moves in big up-and-down swoops like a roller coaster, but he only flashes near the bottom of a swoop and part of the way back up. His trail of light looks like a "J" traced in the air.

When a female spots the pattern of a male of her own species, she flashes in response. If the male sees her lights, he finds her and they mate. If he doesn't see her, he keeps flying and flashing, and the female waits for another male to come by.

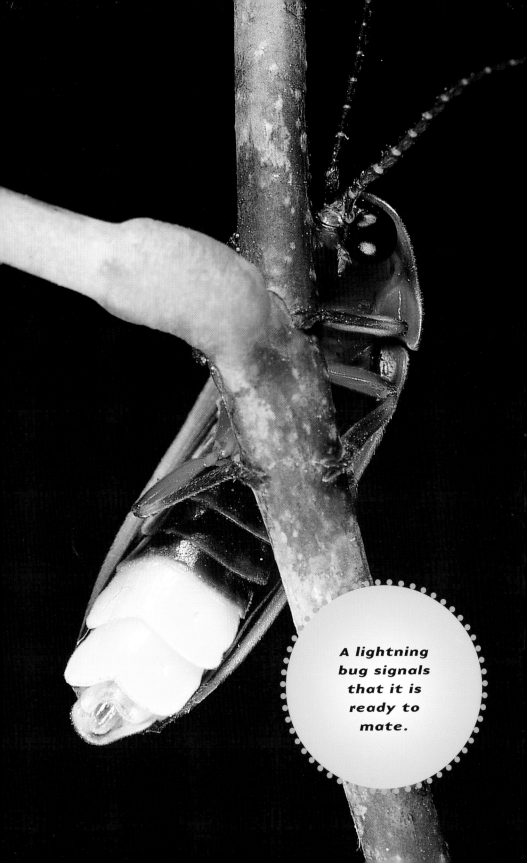

A lightning
bug signals
that it is
ready to
mate.

Are all spiders venomous?

● ● ● ● ● ● ● ● ● ● ● ● ● ●

Is it dangerous to have spiders living in my house?

All spiders make venom that paralyzes or kills their prey, but few spiders can badly hurt people with their bite. In the United States and Canada, deaths from spider bites are very rare. The main spiders you have to watch out for in North America are the black widow and the brown recluse. Black widows are about a half-inch (13 mm) long. They're glossy black with a bright red hourglass marking on the belly. They usually live outdoors and hang their webs from woodpiles or trash heaps. Brown recluse spiders are about the same size as black widows, but they are dull brown, with a wavy stripe down the back. They usually live indoors, in closets or behind furniture.

The brown recluse (above) and black widow (right) are the most dangerous spiders in North America.

It's not dangerous at all to have other kinds of spiders in your house. You might not want them under your pillow or in your underwear drawer, but a quiet little spider in a corner of the room won't hurt you, and it might even help. One small spider can kill hundreds of mosquitoes and other bothersome insects in its lifetime.

What do I do if a spider bites me?

Don't squash the spider! This is probably the opposite of what your first impulse will be. But if it's squashed, you won't be able to tell what kind of spider it was, and that's important. Instead, try trapping it under a glass or jar. Then slide a card under the opening to keep the spider in the jar, and take it to your doctor for identification. If the spider is a dangerous species, your doctor will know how to treat you. If it isn't, your bite will heal in a few days. It might sting and itch, but you will be fine.

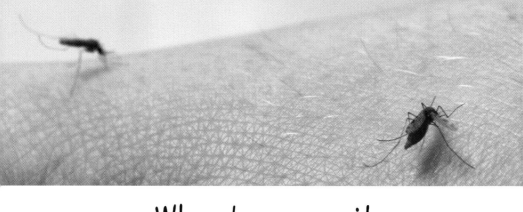

Why do mosquito bites itch?

●●●●●●●●●●●●●●

Has anyone ever died from a mosquito bite?

Mosquito bites itch because the mosquito injects a little of its saliva when it bites you. The saliva contains a chemical that keeps your blood from clotting, so the mosquito can take a good long drink. Your body has an allergic reaction to the saliva, which is what causes the itch. Just as some people are allergic to peanuts or ragweed, some are very sensitive to mosquito bites. They itch for days after being bitten. Other people hardly feel mosquito bites at all.

There's no record that anyone was ever so allergic to mosquito bites that they died from them. However, mosquitoes can spread serious and even deadly diseases. When a carrier mosquito bites you, it injects bacteria, viruses, or other disease-causing organisms along with its saliva. Some of the diseases spread by mosquito bites are malaria and yellow fever, which kill more than a million people a year in tropical parts of the world. These diseases rarely occur in North America. Mosquito-borne diseases can infect other animals, too. The West Nile Virus usually isn't fatal for people, but it does kill horses and birds.

The mosquito's piercing mouth part is called a beak.

Why do some people die from a bee sting?

Bees inject venom when they sting, but that's not what kills people. Just as with mosquito bites, it's an allergic reaction that causes the problem. Very few people are so allergic to bee venom that one sting would kill them. Bees are dangerous because they sometimes gang up on their enemies. If a hive is disturbed, hundreds of bees will swarm out to attack the intruder. Even if you're not especially allergic to bee venom, if you're stung by hundreds of bees at one time, you will be in serious trouble.

Are butterflies and moths the only insects that start out as caterpillars and end up as adults that can fly?

Not at all. Flies, fleas, beetles, and bees also go through complete metamorphosis, like moths and butterflies do. Metamorphosis means "change," and these insects change so much that the adults don't look or act anything like their young. The young, which are called larvae, have tiny legs and no wings. They eat a lot and grow quickly. As they grow, a new, larger exoskeleton forms inside the old one. The new exoskeleton is flexible and folded so it can fit inside. Eventually, the larva gets so big that it molts, or sheds, its old exoskeleton. Then the new exoskeleton can spread out to its full size.

Each larva molts several times as it grows. When it gets big enough, it stops eating and becomes a pupa. This is sometimes called a "resting stage," because the pupa may not move for months. But just because we can't see anything happening on the outside doesn't mean there's nothing going on. Inside, the pupa is working very hard. Its whole body changes shape. The adult will have wings and long legs. Even its mouth and stomach change, because the adult will eat different foods than the larva ate.

Other insects, including dragonflies, crickets, and cockroaches, don't change so much as they grow up. They go through incomplete metamorphosis. Their young are called nymphs if they live on land, like crickets, and naiads if they live in water, like dragonflies. Most nymphs and naiads resemble their parents except that they're smaller and their wings aren't fully grown yet. They don't go through a pupal stage.

What's the difference between butterflies and moths?

Butterflies and moths are close cousins, but they're not too hard to tell apart. If it's flying around in the daytime and has thin antennae

This chrysalis is a pupa that will soon become a butterfly.

with knobs on the ends, it's a butterfly. If it's active in the evening or at night and has thin or feathery antennae without knobs, it's a moth. You can even tell whether a pupa will become a butterfly or a moth. A moth pupa is covered by a papery cocoon. A butterfly pupa, which is also called a chrysalis, isn't wrapped in a cocoon. It stays bare.

Inside this silken cocoon (bottom) is a pupa that will become a moth.

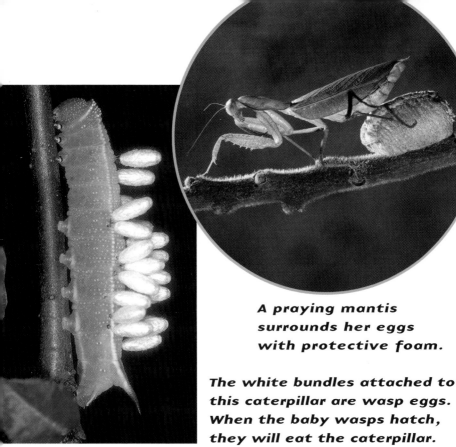

A praying mantis surrounds her eggs with protective foam.

The white bundles attached to this caterpillar are wasp eggs. When the baby wasps hatch, they will eat the caterpillar.

Do insect and spider parents take care of their babies?

Insect and spider mothers help their babies get off to a good start by making sure they will have enough to eat. Some species do this by laying their eggs in a place where the young will find food as soon as they hatch. After they lay their eggs, these mothers die.

Other species stay with their eggs and young to protect them from predators and provide food. Cricket mothers guard their eggs and young nymphs in a burrow. A mother wolf spider carries her young—all 100 of them!—on her back for about a week after they hatch. When they get big enough to hunt, they hop off and start life on their own. Later the mother spider will mate again and have more young.

One thing insect and spider mothers don't do is teach their babies. Their offspring already know how to do everything they will have to do to survive. Young spiders even know how to make perfect webs. They act by instinct, which is behavior they are born with. The good thing about instinct is that it's reliable. It always makes the animal act in a certain way. The bad thing about instinct is that it doesn't let the animal act any other way. So, young insects and spiders do fine as long as their environment remains pretty much the same. But if they face a new situation, they can't think their way through it. They must keep doing what their instincts tell them to do.

How long do bugs live?

Most insects and spiders don't live more than one or two years. A housefly is really old at three weeks of age! Among insects, the life-span champions are the 17-year cicadas, whose nymphs live underground for—you guessed it—

This adult cicada lived underground for many years and is now ready for a short life above ground.

17 years. When they are ready to become adults, they crawl up on a tree trunk and try out their new, full-size wings. They find mates, and the females lay their eggs in shrubs or trees. Then they die. Seven weeks later, the eggs hatch, and the new nymphs drop to the ground. They dig into the soil and won't see daylight again for 17 years.

Among spiders, female tarantulas and trapdoor spiders live longest, up to 25 years. Their mates live only a few years. Most male spiders die soon after they mate for the first time.

Where do bugs go in winter?

Most adult insects and spiders don't even try to live through winter. They die as soon as the weather turns cold, leaving behind eggs or young that can survive the harsh season. Praying mantises surround their eggs with insulating foam that keeps them safe until spring. Most moths and butterflies are in their caterpillar or pupal stage in winter. In a few species the adults fly away to warmer places. Monarch butterflies are the most famous insect migrators, but not the only ones. Potato leafhoppers, which are only an eighth of an inch (3 mm) long, fly from the northern United States to Central America in the fall.

A few insects and spiders don't mind cold weather. They have antifreeze chemicals in their bodies so they can stay active at low temperatures. But many more species just wait for the cold to pass. They snuggle under fallen leaves, burrow into the ground, or find sheltered nooks in old, rotting logs. Then they stop moving. When the temperature warms up again, they will slowly begin to straighten and bend their legs, getting the kinks out after their long winter's nap.

Monarch butterflies travel hundreds of miles to their winter homes in California and Mexico.

I once saw a cookbook with recipes for bugs. Do people really eat those things?

You bet! In many parts of the world, people rely on insects and spiders as a major source of protein. Bug bodies contain three times more protein than lean beefsteak. If you lived in southern Africa, you might snack on crispy dried caterpillars. In Bali, you could order stir-fried dragonflies. In Southeast Asia, you could buy a barbecued tarantula on a stick and, after polishing off your tasty treat, use the spider's fangs as toothpicks.

It's not a good idea to taste bugs you find around the house or yard, though. If they're the wrong kinds, or aren't cleaned and cooked properly, they can make you sick. If you really want to try eating bugs, watch for a special event sponsored by a nature center or college near your home.

When they're roasted, these beetles will make a crunchy, high-protein snack.

Is it true that old poop would pile up around us if insects disappeared?

Yes, we could be in it up to our knees if dung beetles disappeared. Ancient Egyptians saw dung beetles roll camel poop into little balls for their young to eat. But no one realized how important

Dung beetles roll a ball of camel poop for their young to eat.

these beetles are until about 100 years ago, when English settlers brought cattle to Australia. Their new country had wide, open spaces, but no dung beetles. So the cattle grazed, and they pooped, and the cow pies piled up—360 million new ones every day. With no dung beetles to help them decompose, the cow pies just stayed there. Finally, someone thought of bringing in dung beetles from Europe and Africa. Within a few years, the runaway dung was under control. (And Australia smelled a whole lot better!)

Carrion beetles like this one help recycle dead animals, just as dung beetles help recycle waste.

OK, we'll keep dung beetles, but couldn't we do without the bugs that bug us the most?

Like dung beetles, all insects and spiders probably help us in some way. We just don't understand how yet. Our supply of chocolate is a good example. People have raised cacao plants for hundreds of years, but we still don't know for sure which insects pollinate them. What if we kept the midges and got rid of the aphids, and then found out it's the aphids that pollinate cacao after all? By then it would be too late.

No, we're better off keeping all the bugs. And not just to pollinate our favorite plants. They also provide chemicals that doctors use to treat epilepsy, stroke, Alzheimer's, and other

Pollen clings to a bee and will be carried to other plants.

**Many birds and frogs depend
on insects for food.**

diseases. They recycle nutrients back into the soil. Many fish, frogs, and birds depend on them for food. Hummingbirds need them for another reason. They hold their tiny nests together with bits of silk they take from nearby spiderwebs.

We may not understand everything insects and spiders do, but that just means we need to keep asking questions about them and learning from them. Besides, what would a summer evening be without the sound of crickets or the flashes of fireflies?

A leaf-cutter ant lugs a leaf back to its nest, a jumping spider watches for prey, and a zodiac moth stops to rest.

tall tales about bugs

You can tell the temperature by counting cricket chirps.

You might have heard that if you count the number of times a cricket chirps in one minute (then subtract 40 from that number, divide by 4, and add 50), that will tell you the temperature (in degrees Fahrenheit). It's a fun story, but it only works for one species, the snowy tree cricket. If you're listening to some other kind of cricket, you might as well just guess at the temperature. Or check a thermometer!

Spiders shoot out their strands of silk.

Only Spiderman does that! Real spiders can't shoot their silk, which comes from holes called spigots located at the spider's hind end. The silk oozes out as a liquid, and then finger-like structures called spinnerets pull on it to stretch it out into a thread. If a spider anchors its new thread to a wall or branch, the strand of silk will be pulled out as the spider walks away or drops toward the ground.

Earwigs got their name because they crawl into people's ears.

This is a superstition that started in Europe hundreds of years ago. Earwigs look creepy, with big pincers called cerci on their tail end. In fact, they are peaceable creatures that live under leaves, in rain gutters, and in gardens. Sometimes, if they're frightened or upset, they squirt a brown fluid that smells awful. But they do not crawl inside people's ears. They are just stuck with a very bad name.

Dragonflies will sew your mouth shut while you're asleep.

They've even been called "devil's darning needles." That's just one of many folk tales about these big, impressive insects. Superstitions also say that dragonflies bring dead snakes back to life, lead good children to good fishing holes, and sting children who've been bad. But dragonflies can't sew, revive snakes, or sting. They can't even bite harder than a pinch. They are superb hunters, though. One dragonfly can eat more than 300 mosquitoes every day, which isn't devilish at all.

resources

BOOKS

DETHIER, VINCENT. *To Know a Fly*. San Francisco: Holden-Day, Inc., 1962.

EVANS, HOWARD ENSIGN. *Life on a Little-Known Planet*. New York: Dutton, 1993.

FOELIX, RAINER F. *Biology of Spiders*. New York: Oxford University Press, 1996.

GORDON, DAVID GEORGE. *The Eat-A-Bug Cookbook*. Berkeley: Ten Speed Press, 1998.

HILLYARD, PAUL. *The Book of the Spider*. New York: Random House, 1994.

HUBBELL, SUE. *Broadsides from the Other Orders*. New York: Random House, 1993.

LEVI, HERBERT W. and LORNA R. *Spiders and Their Kin*. New York: Golden Press, 1987.

MASON, ADRIENNE. *The World of the Spider*. San Francisco: Sierra Club Books, 1999.

WALDBAUER, GILBERT. *Insects Through the Seasons*. Cambridge, MA: Harvard University Press, 1996.

WEB SITES

www.arachnology.org
This is the official Web site of the Arachnology Society, where you can learn all about spiders. Click on the Arachnology pages and follow the link to the Kids' page.

www.billybear4kids.com/butterfly/flutter-fun.html
This site has lots of games and activities about butterflies and even flash cards you can print out to test your butterfly knowledge.

www.insecta-inspecta.com
Learn about arachnophobia, insects on coins and stamps, and lots of other fun facts. You can also enter an insect art contest.

www.monarchwatch.org
Follow the monarch butterflies on their yearly migrations at this site hosted by the University of Kansas Entomology Program.

www.npwrc.usgs.gov/resource/distr/lepid/bflyusa/bflyusa.htm
Click on your state to find out what butterflies live there, or follow a trail of photos to identify butterflies you find.

www.seps.org/cvoracle/faq/spiders.html
Identify a bug you've caught and find answers to all your insect and spider questions. This site is hosted by Science Education Partnerships and has great ideas for your teachers, too.

www.uky.edu/Agriculture/Entomology/ythfacts/entyouth.htm
This site, called "Katerpillars (and Mystery Bugs)," offers tips on collecting bugs, how to make insect ornaments, a mystery bug for you to identify, and more. It even explains why they misspelled "Katerpillar."

www.urbanext.uiuc.edu/bugreview/index_name.html
"The Bug Review" from the University of Illinois gives pictures and information on many different species of insects. You can search by bug name or by region.

http://bugscope.beckman.uiuc.edu
A Webcam at this site lets students control the camera to go nose-to-nose with flies, cockroaches, and other insects.

http://www.extremescience.com/BiggestBug.htm
This site by "Extreme Science" features the Goliath Beetle, the biggest bug in the world.

http://www.insects.org
To see how people throughout the world celebrate their passion for bugs, check out this Web site called "Bug Bios."

http://whyfiles.org/016skeeter/index.html
"Mosquito Bytes" is a Web site devoted to spreading information about disease-spreading mosquitoes.

http://yucky.kids.discovery.com
Click on "Roach World" for cool roach trivia. Did you know that most roaches have 18 knees? There are fascinating (and disgusting) facts on other "yucky" bugs, too!

About the Author

CHERIE WINNER WRITES BOOKS AND ARTICLES FOR children and adults. Her favorite subjects are animals and plants, and the people who study them. Several of her books have been named Outstanding Science Trade Books for Children. Dr. Winner has taught college classes, done research on salamanders, and worked as a newspaper reporter. Nowadays, when she isn't writing about nature, she enjoys creating mini-habitats in her yard to attract insects, spiders, snakes, and birds. This puzzles her dog Sheba and cat Smudge, but they are good sports about it.

Tammy Medsker

Do you have questions about other animals? We want to hear from you! E-mail us at **kidsfaqs@creativepub.com.** For more details, log on to **www.northwordpress.com.**